Bricked Bats

Other Work

Between Islands (1984)

Standing Room (1989)

Before Arguable Answers (1993)

Sky Open Again (1997)

Of All the Corners to Forget (2004)

Aid & A_Bet (2008)

Who Lets Go First (2010)

Machines We Have Built (2014)

Bricked Bats

Gian Lombardo

A ClearSound book from Quale Press

Acknowledgment is made to where some of the work herein has previously appeared: "Holding Pattern," "Roll Over" & "Broken," *Laurel Review;* "The Yard (& Beyond)," "Devil of a Time" & "From the Garden," *Sentence;* "Recipe for Disaster," *Inscape;* "Little Universes," *untitled: a magazine of prose poetry* and in *Alcatraz: International Anthology of Prose/Poetry*; "Dialog of Exchange," *Montague Reporter;* "Petal to the Metal," *MiPoesias;* "Sequestered Alliances," *Quarter After Eight;* "Sins of Omniscience," *DMQ Review.* "Equations," "Lack of Direction," "Yet Another Set of Sexual Practices," "Some Residuals of the Cardinal Sins" & "Phases," appeared in the Red Pagoda Press pamphlet series. Many thanks are given to the editors of these publications.

ISBN: 978-1935835-28-8
LCCN: 2021943933
Cover: *Abandoned House, North Poland Road, Conway, Mass.*, photo by Gian Lombardo

Contents

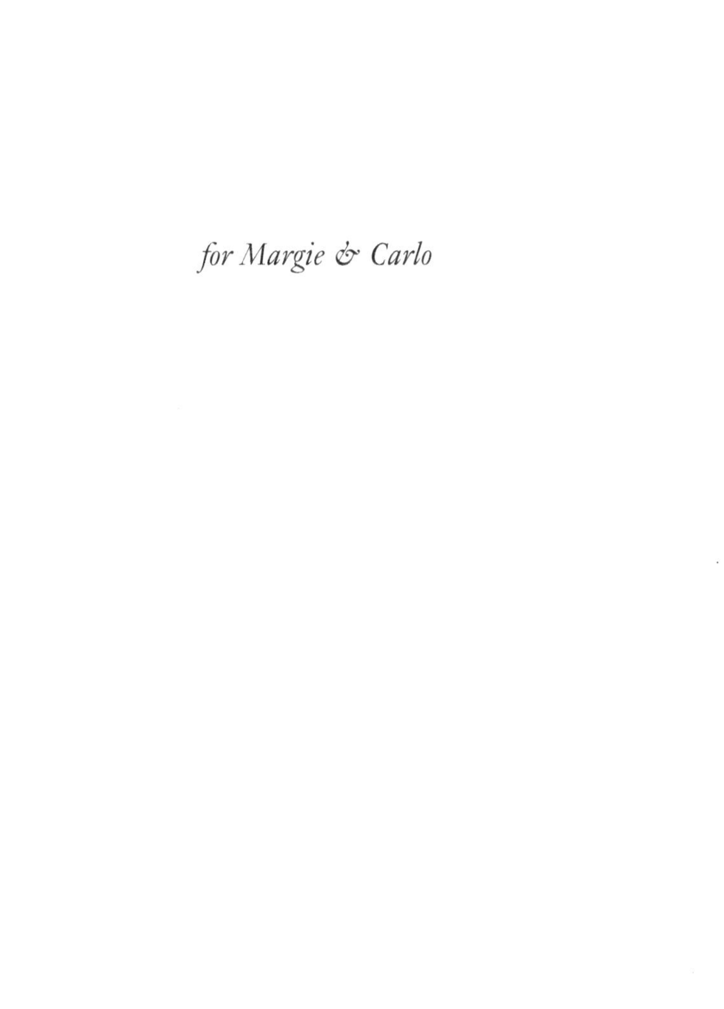

for Margie & Carlo

Little Universes

Little Universes

Sitting in a corner of the lobby, turning the pages of a magazine. It's been long, too long, but not so long that introductions are needed.

Who else is looking? It might not matter. In this resort, no one goes there alone to be alone, nor does anyone go there without having made prior arrangements.

Not that there might be someone, on a whim, or a dare, who walks up to the desk, fresh from the evening's last train, betting on finding something open.

That's what's counted on, the flint struck, setting a glow of sparks.

But then travelers share much in common, so many cogs engaging teeth, so many gears meshing.

Such rueful glances, and if they turn bold? All the accumulated tensions of motion are drained upon arrival.

What if it were the wind that rattled the windows, negotiating the corridors joining room to room despite the walls?

(What transpires, inspires.)

The furtive knocks for entrance into exquisite intimate clubs, secret handshakes. And if someone's not seen, moving from hall to hall, around this corner and that, slipping, hopefully, unnoticed into a doorway.

Or the remains of a scent, distilled in air, or minor indentation in a plush carpet? What does that signal?

If seen or unseen? Significant, or other? Above, with unsleeping eye, playing checkmate with the hope of the best vantage point.

As always, a game played best to at least one player's benefit.

All those doors closing as softly as possible. And the occasional errant slam. Who best to wake? Or is this hotel grounds for a vast hide-and-seek?

Sunk in a corner, peering from behind an overstuffed armchair, a child's face.

For a moment, the mouth breaks as if to unleash a tongue or a smile. Instead, abruptly, a hand appears next to the curly hair, waving.

So much the perfect gesture: What else describes both coming and going?

Ordonnance

An old laugh. A laugh that could have come from someone old.

An empty car. All four doors open wide. Even trunk and hood lifted.

From the edge of the road a sitting figure with one leg tucked under the other bent at the knee, foot firmly planted on the shoulder. The knee serves as a rest for a rifle.

Pointed at an expanse strewn with corn stubble, a shot rings out and echoes back.

Crows scatter, taking refuge in trees rimming one side of the field.

An old, odd laugh. A laugh that could have come from someone who's had it, or had the hell of it.

Rifle placed on the ground, a jacket collar gets pulled up, sheltering neck against wind.

A long line of broken clouds rushes above the cawing of the crows toward a reddening horizon.

Fallen. Fallen out. Fallen in with arms open to a harsh wind.

One crow returns to field. Stock to shoulder, barrel braced against knee.

Stretch a black vault over the clouds. Confuse the sound of shot and door slam.

A laugh as if trained in oratory. A laugh in punctuation of the insistence on scraps.

In the scatter begins the beginning of the end of the pilgrimage.

Overtone

"Dressed all in white, except for a black belt. And, yes, the blue string tie. I can't tell you how wonderful it was to have that come off."

"The only thing is that I couldn't reach the glass in time. It seemed like ages, tilting over the edge of the table, spinning end over end. Let me tell you I was surprised as you were. But I am sorry I couldn't help it from waking you."

"Is it really necessary to be poor? Couldn't we be middling or fair?"

"Here, I think this pencil must belong to you."

"No, maybe you do resemble her after all. I mean there are some things you've picked up along the way. Like how when you're lost for words you bring your hand to your cheek and your thumb rests against the underside of your chin."

"I don't know if we should go any further. I don't know what that is."

"Rubberized accessories have been our downfall. Pure and simple."

"No wonder I couldn't get anywhere. First, with that hell-in-a-handbag stuff and then with all that digging. No way it didn't get on my nerves. There I was, stuck. Without a clue when all I wanted was to get revved up."

"Later on you'll thank me. That's just how it is."

"As if passed by, but not forgotten. There was something too good about that."

"My, how pretty. Can we do the exchange now?"

"And when they hatch, you just have to laugh. There's nothing else you can do. Everything's still, then suddenly everything's filled with these silent-movie pratfalls."

Dialog of Exchange

Perhaps I have entered the line. At its end due to an insistence on politeness. The affront would be to enter somewhere further up. If someone stares, it's ignored. The same goes for any exclamations. Sure, I know what I've done. What of it?

But did I do it? Let's go back to the end of this beginning and wait.

At the front of the line, some articles are placed on the counter. I'm so far back, I can't make out exactly what they are. Others in line do not pay attention.

I try to look elsewhere but there's not much. There's not even someone behind me. Yet. I expect company to approach my back soon.

The suspense might kill me as the line inches forward. From further up I hear humming. Then what sounds like cymbals, or maybe little bells.

It's a pretty sound. Similar to the ring of an old typewriter when it reaches the end of a line. But I'm still far from the counter.

I'm sure, though, it's not from a clock. What clock chimes almost every minute?

I've noticed a correlation: A flurry of music and the line moves shortly thereafter.

There are other concurrences: The aforementioned articles, sometimes just one, placed on the counter. After the chime, the person behind the counter extends a hand. Something gets dropped into the hand. Last, the articles, those seen before, or maybe one, disappear.

Whomever's at the head of the line also walks away. They mostly hurry, clutching a grubby bag.

I begin to think there's a conspiracy. There should be a mountain of things on the counter and it's clean as can be.

I picked up what's in my hand because I like them. Enough to stand in line.

Above Fact

Someone's playing dice with my bones. I'd say I'm all sixes and sevens, but it's hard to tell with all the commotion.

It started with that old feeling and just grew. Maybe a spell cast from that bag of old black magic.

Or a black bag of that magic. Who cares? What's important is that ache, that twinge like it was going to rain from here to forever.

(Only thing is, it didn't rain. The only thing that wet my face was that feeling of rain.)

But who cares about the color of magic when everything's a jumble?

Tell me when I come up snake eyes. Remember: Eyes, not tongue. Tell me when I pass to the next gambler. Maybe I'll be lucky then.

Close your eyes and breathe. Let it roll.

Recipe for Disaster

Is this the one with too much salt? Or was it too much metal shavings?

Having it come out right is crucial. There's no room for error.

If error enters, something else must leave. Two objects occupying the same space would be pushing it.

Unless that arrangement were considered cozy. In that case, error enters, gets closer, closer, tries to squeeze in, keeps deflecting all talk on what it might be up to. . .

Holding Pattern

The cylinder loose way above the clouds. What goes up? It must. Keep up.

No fences or leashes in that realm. There. Above. If anything, it runs free. That's it. Free ride.

If only it goes up as it should come down. Down as it follows up. Down right. Up right.

Take off the landing and what do you get? Embarrassed, or turned to on. On mark. Ride on.

Against the fear of height, the fright of falling. Hand in hand. Free fall. For keeps.

And here a foot presses on, right up against the horizon.

Sequestered Alliances

Which of these statements warrants further investigation?

The black pen lays perpendicular to the keyboard on the desk.

After much effort he managed to walk everywhere backwards without crashing into anything.

There are usually nine pigeons on the roof. Today, there's ten.

The broccoli in last night's curry was, in a previous life, a squirrel that had gnawed its way into a friend's attic.

If the water was so calm, how come nothing could be seen more than an arm's reach under water?

Of course, outside the window there's another, wider world. In this case, there's some relief it's never been caught looking in.

Petal to the Metal

Aluminum's jealous of lead. The malleability. The heaviness.

But then gold's envious of aluminum. It's almost everywhere, nearly as common as flies. Gold wants to be held by the many, not the few.

(But we won't venture onto an analysis of gold's leanings to satyriasis.)

Will gold and lead ally against aluminum? The dross and the pure, as it were.

Is this a modern fairy tale (or alchemist's wet dream) or what? Lead knocking on gold's door, bearing chocolates. . . Gold answering the door, arms full of flowers. . .

Leading the Way

The wind moved among the trees like some child playing peek-a-boo.

The kid stood behind one tree and only darted behind another when all was clear, like a criminal on the lam.

The fugitive took great pains to survey the whole scene, looking front and back and right and left before making a move, as a hawk would, scouring a field for a mouse.

The bird of prey, ever alert, swiftly dove, forsaking the drafts bent skyward as they struck the meadow's forested edge.

Lock
Book Look

Eyes Have Had It

Night ignited by sharp cracks of branches laden with ice. And the long drag of ice scurrying across ice. A rattling exhale.

=

In the pitch there were once three. Then two. And the sound of sliding gravel.

=

Yawled arias from whatever wants a handout. Taken in a bowl, full of white.

=

Moonless dark and dark drop off. Anti-life wavers in the sheer face, calling, whispering, chilling. Eyes close towards something. Or else.

=

Rocks weep with forgiveness. They ignore prayers. Ignore bouts of license. What's doubtful can find another way out as others go in.

=

Temper the pause between cracks with the sound of the frozen breathing of the storm. Past the afternoon poling upriver. Past forgetting rembering the passage of time. And the theft of dark elderberries hanging into the flow.

Eagleville Pond

Broken

The bones are not my idea. My idea of bones is the story of how you'd bring some carcass — a mole, sparrow, chipmunk, rabbit — and your idea of a gift would result in its relocation.

o

The spruce windbreak, the rocks under the sugar maples — the places that would receive the gifts were also your idea of hiding places or places to scout and replenish the stock.

o

Whose idea is the idea of a house surrounded by piles of delicate bones?

o

—What was named to break never broke what governs the movement of gifts from wakeful hunt to a hunted disappearance.—

o

Even the longest absence turns on its back and demands the idea of a scratch on its belly, reducing comfort to the idea of watching an idea sleep.

East Guinea Road

—*for K.S.*

No Fouls

Bare rocks finger absence. Between high water and forest floor.

¤

Deer hooves litter the interstitial zone. Draining sparks from an abandoned fire. Drained from an imaginary evening.

¤

A safe moment of sand carved into the facets of the back of a hand. Or the curse of the small of a back.

¤

Tide arrives, restless. But quiet from the journey.

¤

Rocks provide shelves. Plateaus with smoothed edges holding the bric-a-brac of what could be snow globes left behind by ordinary divinities.

¤

For all the wildness of the whiteness there are forgotten lifts of sound from the branches. What we have missed most was bird prattle.

¤

Marsh grass pantomimes wind, furious it's an effect. And the warmth exits sand for atmosphere.

Watts Island

Drawing Fields

Nestled in the crook of an arm, the flow shallows give way to a vocal pool edged by a small spit of sand.

+

Flow, a swimmer swimming.

+

Someone could sit behind the curtain of water and pretend to slap Punchinello. Or take issue with soliloquies.

+

No one mistakes the sound for laughter. Or applause.

+

The bridge attracted castabouts. One lonesome fury tried to throw itself off. Another, a fistful of rubber flew into the air and landed a myth none could find trace of.

+

One bend knelt at the foot of a wide oval mound of earth.

+

If one could play the flow, it could only be done by ear. Subtle variations of a motif that could not be mastered in one humid afternoon.

+

Corn populated the wide plain. Silk rustling — like skirts even without wind.

+

Harvest theft of rot.

Konkapot River

Steps V

Wet sparks burn against concrete — this thin curtain of detonations behind which players assemble, mark position, get ready to speak what's never been heard.

§

Branches rise and fall in waves announcing the wind at the head of the gorge.

§

A narrow sluice flicks a rooster tail into a rock-lined basin. Over the spray, an arm almost bridges the gap. Over the pool, a fallen hemlock spans from rock wall to rock wall. Everywhere, trees criss-cross riverbed, trailbed.

§

Never resting too long in the bottoms of the stone-bowls, brown spots leap against the twisting vein of white. Here and there the tumbling current swallows a pocket of air. Each cascade voices its own signature sound.

§

One the far side, in a smaller, shaded ravine, the quiet trickle of water rises from deep in aching rock.

§

Shadow moves from one bank to the other. A brown spider moves from its perch at end of a log. Overhead, for a moment, from a slivered sky caught between a net of trees, sunlight reflects against a shelf of grey stone.

§

At the bottom of the gorge, the remains of an old rock wall guards the penultimate basin. The wide iron pipe that once ferried water to the wheel burnishes the bank with rust.

§

Now the wind arrives at the final, sandy pool. Millions of warm exhalations of the most commonly forgotten words tender every inch of skin. Here, with nothing left untouched by sun, the

body chooses to speak only with cool water
against back and belly, a hand slapping reflections
on the water's surface — its own note of applause.

South River Dam

The Burden of Cause

Nothing Doing

Bird one flies onto a branch. The branch sags slightly under its weight. It bends closer to the ground.

On the ground a squirrel senses the new nearness of the branch and, of course, bird one.

Bird two flies onto the same branch, which bends even more.

The squirrel approaches the tree's trunk. It's time to scale.

Bird three lands on the branch. It's getting nearer to the earth.

The squirrel thinks about leaping up onto the branch, but thinks better and shoots up the trunk.

The squirrel has to think better: There's a cat on its trail.

Pretty soon we have many birds in the tree. Some are on the branch. Some are on other branches.

(Did you notice if it was raining? Birds, squirrel and cat dodging a shower.)

Of all the inhabitants of the tree, the squirrel is the only one jumping from branch to branch.

The cat's more careful. It strides slowly, always looking for the shortest way to the squirrel.

Many birds now feel uneasy: They are aware of squirrel and cat. They are ready for anything until the squirrel leaps and with a crack the branch breaks.

The squirrel tumbles to the ground, that branch never closer to terra firma than it is now, until some of the many birds who are ready for anything decide to spread their wings out again on plain air.

Sins of Omniscience

I don't know why I didn't tell you before. It must have slipped my mind.

Think of it as: What you don't know can't hurt you.

That is, until now.

But I could always back away, lose the train of thought, or hope for a sudden change of topic like the wind dropping to a standstill right before the storm.

Nothing stirs in the eerie silence.

Or was it looking into the eye of the hurricane? Everything flying this way and that way and, then, whap, stuck face-to-face with an unexpected lull. Why even the sun breaks out for a moment.

You know how to fill those lulls, no hemming or hawing, just like in the movies where you'd have no idea it took them two-dozen tries to let that pause curl up and die.

Who Says What

Enough said: Just edge back from going over the top.

Well put: A place for everything and everything in its place.

Stay put: Never let the genie escape.

But rub two wishes together:

Now that's talking.

To Stand On

Just off to the side. That's the way I prefer to appear in photos.

Maybe looking off to the side, searching for something outside the frame.

Caught between glass and cardboard, between a rock and a hard place.

(If only the glass were of the looking kind.)

Knock against glass, seeking an out. Beside myself, pacing in confinement, pulling at the chain.

And, what remains of a foot, although not quite in the picture, chewed to release the shackle.

One-Track Mind

I watch the trains go by. These days, I'm content to listen and not even turn my head to catch the flash of a silver car.

I don't envy those who are going somewhere. I am somewhere and, for a moment, they are rushing pell-mell towards me.

But, don't worry, a train's never hit me.

All those close calls: The feel of the wind stirred by that moving mass. Vibrations leaving the ground and traveling up my limbs.

There's something about the attraction of a much larger object. In this case, a much faster object.

It's true, too, they sound different coming and going. And once one passes, all that lingers pares down to a low, rumbling moan.

Roll Over

They say dogs can hear an earthquake before we do. Or possibly feel the vibrations of rock colliding and breaking.

Suddenly, the sleeping dog wakes and barks. Or the calm dog striding alongside cowers and whimpers.

Then, the torrent of sound. As if some large, fast-moving object fell out of the sky. All you can do is lunge about on all fours.

No one believes the sky's falling. But you have fallen. (And the earth?)

They also say dogs can see ghosts. Even recognize their faces, movements. Possibly speak in their own way with them. Maybe, if friendly, expect them to bring food.

You wonder. Who says these things? Who has stories to fill with such details?

Sing Along

Sometimes your head's so heavy, you can't keep it straight. Your chin digs into your chest, mouth open in the hope something will come out.

You present an array of virtual speechlessness, the aura of the clogged drain.

The more water, the more weight bears against the plug. All that volume forming an impression on the trap.

But another sheet crowds the next before the ink dries. All those letters and words, smeared one on top of the other.

What else than an illegible book portraying an expanse of nothing out of something, a wide reach aping an aria's held note? Or the breathless scream of the condemned as the door falls away.

All Fall Down

Once up, the inevitable follows. But you hope for the exception. The sailing forever onward, with nothing marking the attainment of full circle.

A long time ago, roundness was the subject of much debate. Later, with debate quieted, circularity seemed a blessing — no fear getting lost, just go straight enough, long enough you'll get to where you came from.

These days you don't fall off the edge and land smack dab where you started.

Where do you land? (Maybe that brings you back to the rule and its desired waiver.)

All those farewells, entrances. And, in the end (or is it the beginning?), how much different is the cessation from the initiation?

Or is the measure the cat's, landing on all fours, brushing off dust and walking away. . .

Remote Perturbations

Three Wishes

To inhabit a word without end. (As if falling, safe in the belief of reaching no ground.)

For the worst that can be dealt: The smile, in equipoise, on either side of a line.

The same willingness to make a mind up when everything chatters in disarray as when the will's made a bed undone by a surfeit of sleep and lovemaking.

Thrashing & Clawing

It's too much being awake. But the alternative, sleep, is far worse. The body, fallen down, struggles against that net. (The body, overthrown, caught, but not still.)

This day had an evil grin. Evil like it would never let go. Who knew it'd lie?

(But so much dark came before. And so much that comes after...)

It's hard. To let go. So much of a good thing.

On Edge

It could be anything: A plosive instead of a liquid. Or a puff of air against the cheek and not the ear.

Then comes the teetering, the careening against the fulcrum when the focus becomes fouled and the near seems far and the far near.

(But that's where it's easy to find one's self lost. And once lost, every point serves as a destination.)

The very sense. Of approaching. The unkindest cut. Knowing any deviation is unavoidable.

From the Garden

The gypsy in the park tries to sell me a plastic flower. She tells me if I buy it, I will save hungry children from starving.

The flower seems too familiar.

I grew up in a house filled with artificial flowers, wax fruit, dead branches stuck in pots of gravel. Everywhere branches littered with the greenery of paper and cloth.

I'm not buying. The gypsy first lowers her price, then curses. May everything I touch turn to dust. Only the lifeless will come to me.

Of course, she didn't need tea leaves.

The Yard (& Beyond)

Dozens of jays zig-zag from tree to tree in the orchard. In a maple, far above them, starlings quarrel: Even though the fruit trees fill with blue some don't believe it's spring.

Under the lawn, moles make the most of the thaw. The cat prowling the grass knows they cannot stay below forever.

In this context I cut back old growth on grape vines and when I return home I bend to clear away tiny rodent skulls from the steps.

Whenever the starlings are quiet, I can hear the stream. On its other bank another hill rises thick with trees.

On the best of days I go into the woods and do not recognize the path I follow along the streambed. In another context my hands are lost to me.

I hang an ornament from a pine tree, careful not to let it drop. Its surface reflects the sky and other trees. If I wore a smile, it would cover a hemisphere.

Splitting the Difference

Equations

Three times know-you-like-a-book divided by the summation of each utterance of you-should-have-known-better.

-- -- --

What passes for love raised to the power of what passes for intellect.

-- -- --

Giggling over the integral of moaning (from pain to ecstasy) less the diffusion of an itch.

-- -- --

The square root of one game, two of clubs, three wise men, five o'clock shadow and eight legs.

-- -- --

Finding the certainty of a single existence divided by two times the shock of discovering metempsychosis is true multiplied by itself times the ratio of the circumference of a soul to its diameter.

-- -- --

Splitting the difference between meaning what you say and saying what you mean.

-- -- --

The aggregate of not taking it lying down and standing up for one's self.

-- -- --

A smile, its width relaxed until its remainder, when contained by a moment of doubt, matches a factor of a laugh.

-- -- --

Lack of Direction

Begin in the east. When you rise, I look your way only to catch a storm blowing in my right ear (and clear out my left).

* * *

It's not enough to give me the cold shoulder. There's even moss growing among my chest hair.

* * *

You just hang there too stubborn and sexy to move. I'd better open the windows. The room's gotten a little bit too small.

* * *

Who painted my face so many colors? I don't know if I should make you laugh or go to war.

* * *

One More Set of Sexual Practices

After a hard life in the circus, you lie down and cry. A small, greenish bird hovers about your face, sipping your tears.

\+ + +

With three sheets to the wind, roll down a hill until your body floats.

\+ + +

One size too small. And so you're returned to the store. Bide your time until someone two sizes too big for you tries to slink their way in.

\+ + +

In line, you can hardly wait for your turn in the spelling bee to come: You've memorized the spelling of every dirty word in your tongue.

\+ + +

You orbit the spindle. Every once in a while the needle sticks and we are treated to the same thrilling passage of notes: A love song with hiccups.

\+ + +

Your fur is rubbed and sparks fly. That's the time to really tap into the current. Stick your finger into an electrical socket.

\+ + +

If coating glue on both surfaces, beware they will never part again.

\+ + +

Some Residuals of the Cardinal Sins

You break out in hives from all those peacock feathers.

~ ~ ~

After humping one of the table legs, it starts wearing condoms.

~ ~ ~

Your neighbors paint their lawns blue.

~ ~ ~

When you speak, your voice is hoarse from the cold breezes of all those people trying to blow out your wick.

~ ~ ~

But you mistakenly think you're a birthday cake. Won't they be surprised if they take a bite?

~ ~ ~

There's so much shit, it can't avoid hitting the fan.

~ ~ ~

If you felt like getting around to it. . .

~ ~ ~

Phases

What can be done when it can be filled no more? Howl for another? Mop the surplus from the floor?

| | |

The face in profile. Slapped, surprise drains its flush and glow. Later, later, the other cheek's turned.

| | |

The sickle against a field of black. What kind of revolution demands a flag like this? Ghosts of the world unite and cast off your chains.

| | |

A blackboard with white streaks and smudges: Remains of problems, shards of answers. Listen for the applause of erasers.

| | |

Ospreys emit a most piteous cry.

quale [kwa-lay]: *Eng.* n 1. A property (such as hardness) considered apart from things that have that property. 2. A property that is experienced as distinct from any source it may have in a physical object. *Ital.* pron.a. 1. Which, what. 2. Who. 3. Some. 4. As, just as.

www.ingramcontent.com/pod-product-compliance
Lightning Source LLC
LaVergne TN
LVHW050941080826
845145LV00004B/1352

* 9 7 8 1 9 3 5 8 3 5 2 8 8 *